The Cimmerian Shade

Kevin Hassing

BookLeaf Publishing

India | USA | UK

The Cimmerian Shade © 2022

Kevin Hassing

All rights reserved.

Presentation by *BookLeaf Publishing*

Web: www.bookleafpub.com

E-mail: info@bookleafpub.com

ISBN: 978-93-5744-445-3

First edition 2022

Jouska

Down the street walked a young confident boy. The boy regarded himself as a polymath. He told people his knowledge was outstandingly broad and that he knew more facts than anyone of his age. A new school year was about to begin, at a new school. The school building was in a terrible state of neglect. He went through the long see-through doors into his next stage of life, which was – according to him – going to be a stage of great success. As he got his first glance of his new life, he noticed something in the building which was rather odd. It seemed that the students were obviously flawed. He went to his first class. In the classroom, the students sat behind their desks, paying attention to nothing else besides their computer. No one had even noticed him entering the classroom. He coughed to catch some attention, however no one seemed to bother. He was surprised, as he was in fact an intruder. He sat down at the desk that was assigned to him. On the desk was a small wooden pencil and a paper with his name written on it with a red marker. Next to him sat a young girl. He analyzed her. She wore a black shirt and a long orange skirt. He tried to count

the pimples on her face. As he looked at her skin
and compared it with his shirt, he came to the
conclusion that her skin needed an ironing.
"Hello, how are you on this fine day?" he said to
her.
She smiled. Her teeth made him think of rotten
cheese: they looked exactly identical.
"I'm doing great, thank you for asking."
She then turned her head back to the computer
and stared blankly at it. The boy was extremely
frustrated by his classmate's disinterest. He
wondered how the conversation could have
gone. She would respond by asking how he was
doing and then show interest by asking him
about who he was. He would be flattered to tell
all the details: about his summer vacation, about
his travel experiences, about his photography
talent, about how he was the best in his class last
year. She would have been greatly impressed by
his many talents and she would have
complimented him by saying, "You are so
inspiring. Your passion motivates me," which
would have given him a jubilant feeling. Yet this
conversation he had played out in his head, was
just his imagination. The young boy had a
ravenous appetite for attention, which he hadn't
gotten. The feeling he had was one of anger and
of much frustration. He sighed loudly and stared
at the paper on which was his name. Vesper the

red letters spelled, a name of a boy who felt
misunderstood.

Monachopsis

She swiftly flew through the air. Her red wings of fire were fully charged. The cold breeze of the wind detached her from her roots of despair. She felt alive. Yet the persistent feeling of loneliness kept raging on. There wasn't anyone who understood her in the forest. She tried to enjoy the company of the trees, the creatures and the seaswan. But they were all too different and had a hard time understanding her complex troubles. Only the clouds were open to hear her feelings. However, the clouds were stubborn and grumpy creatures on which she couldn't rely. The harsh attitude they showed always made her cry – inside. Though she had to admit that she admired their honesty. One day she went up to the cloud which was shaped most like a sea turtle.

"I wondered how life is in the human world?" she asked.

The cloud darkened from a bright white to a severe gray.

"Roc, never talk about those filthy creatures," the cloud barked, "They pollute, they kill, there is just too much that they spill."

But still she was interested in those wingless people. They lived in a world which was changing constantly, something her little world did not. Roc had the feeling she was going back in time living in the forest. Yet she knew there was a great danger with those humans which should be left alone. As the clouds had told her, humans had awarely demolished the earth into complete destitution. Humans had slain each and every creature just for their own appetite as they enjoyed licking every inch of the bone. Smog had been released into the air by those humans, causing great pollution. Nonetheless, she had been feeling the need to ghost in that world. And though that feeling kept haunting in her head, she ignored it.

As she sat down on a rock, near a bright shiny lake, she watched the water flow. And though she admired the beauty of the lake, her thoughts were flooding with anguish. Roc tried to get up quickly. But then she tripped on a rock and was assured: she was out of place. Life didn't feel like a rollercoaster, but much more like a snail race to her. The pressure behind her eyes rose to an absolute maximum and before she knew it, tears streamed down her cheek. And there Roc lay, fallen on the green grass, weak.

Chrysalism

Vesper got home from his long day at school. He put his shoes away and went straight to the kitchen. There he encountered his mother with her green jewel. It was an emerald necklace that she wore to show off her wealth. His father was sitting at the table with a glass of beer. He was an alcoholic with bad health. Vesper made eye-contact with his father. As a first response he smiled.

"Do you need something?" His father fumed.

"No, I'm terribly sorry," Vesper answered in a soft voice.

His father was a terrible man. Vesper longed to be loved by his family, yet that was just a dream of him. He remembered one time when he had taken a hurt bee with him home. Vesper took care of the bee as its wings were broken. Yet as his father found out about the bee, he smashed it to its grave, which left Vesper heartbroken. Despite the awful creature his father was, Vesper did feel sorry for him. It was the alcohol that had been sending him down the wrong path. The hundreds of beers he had drunk had not just turned him into a grim figure, but into a complete psychopath.

"Go ahead and make yourself comfortable, spoiled little brat!" his father sassed as Vesper sat down on the chair near the window. Vesper looked outside the window: it was raining cats and dogs. The raindrops on the window he found fascinating. He followed how every raindrop landed on the window and how it made its way down. As he was focusing on a raindrop gliding down, thunder struck in the corner of his eye. He peered in the distance when lightning struck once more. A loud bang followed from the sky. And then he waited patiently for lightning to strike again, waiting for the climax. The excitement he felt during the thunderstorm converted into a feeling of peace. He was once not aware of his father non stop shouting at him – just the sound of thunder was able to make its way to his ears.

Earth

The clouds had told Roc a lot about the existence of the awful creatures called humans. Humans were the monsters of the planet and whatever Roc did, she had to stay away from them. The humans would find her fascinating and use her for their own purposes. She had been told three short horror stories about humans.

The first one was about earth. One day a group of humans settled in the forest, looking innocent. The humans befriended the trees. One day, one tree and a human had become such good friends that the tree dared to tell the human a secret. The tree told him about a tree of life in the forest which balanced the magic of nature. Yet, in contrast to what the tree had expected, the human went to the tree of life to burn it down, by which all the magic of nature died. Some time later the human came back to his tree friend. His tree friend begged him to reverse what he had done, yet the human brutally burned down his tree friend.

Dead Reckoning

Roc was walking through the forest seeking for the most beautiful flowers. She took every different coloured flower she could find with her, from a pure yellow buttercup to a warm orange chrysanthemum. As Roc reached for a beautiful marigold, a crow snapped it out of her hand. The crow took the flower with him on a branch, tore the flower up in pieces and then flew away. Roc remained calm and continued on with her flowersearch. After a while she got back home after a long day. She lived in the ruïnes of an old abandoned castle. To cheer the place up she put the beautiful flowers down she had collected. She had been living in the castle all alone for as long as she could remember. When the night fell, Roc went for a flight in the cold air. The auburn sky brought her into a coma state of mindfulness. She felt thankful for the euphonious sounds of nature: the wind blowing through the trees, the waves of the lakes, the singing of the birds. But when kraa sounded, the mindful state died. It was a crow which had turned the tide. It wasn't just any crow: it was the flower destroying crow. The kraa sounded at her castle down on the ground. And so, she flew right back to face her foe. Nevertheless, she was too late. All the beautiful flowers she had collected had been eaten and torn up by the black bird.

The next day the black bird came back, sitting on a piece of rock while holding a white peony in his beak. Roc hesitated at first, squeezing in her cheek. But then the crow laid the peony down and he flew away. Roc took the peony and held it tightly. She wanted to thank the crow, so she decided to look for her black foe in the air. She looked right in the sun which was shining brightly, and there she saw a black bird in the distance, soaring through the air at full speed. It was a beautiful sighting at first, yet that soon changed due to an awful deed. A gunfire was shot right at the black bird, shooting him right out of the air, getting torn up into pieces. A small black feather was the only thing which was still floating. Roc flew back to her ruïnes and sat down on a rock with the white peony in her hand. Darkness had entered her land. She sniffed the soft sweet peony and cried for the loss of her black feathered friend.

Vemdalen

Vesper went for a little adventure in the woods. He loved photography and there was no better place for that than the forest. In his opinion, every photo had its own story and that's what made photos unique. Photos showed life and a magic that wasn't weak. The woods were the perfect place to make a record of life. It had just rained and the leaves were still soaking wet, which somehow gave a very homely and secure feeling. Vesper took a photo from up close a leaf with water drops slowly dripping off. He looked at the photo and was proud at first – the pure see-through color of the raindrop appeared even more heavenly on the camera – but the photo wasn't original. Hundreds or even thousands of identical photographs were already existing in the world. Vesper's mind drifted off when he took notice of a beautiful red rose in the dirt. It was the only rose on the grassfield. He photographed the rose, which stood there like a queen who had power to wield. But once again, he wasn't being original. A million identical roses could be found on the internet. He realized photographing life was useless. No authentic photo could express his creativity, not even one

of a silhouette. He had to think outside the box.
He took out a gun from his backpack, peered at a
faraway silhouette and released the bullet into
the sunlight, a glare.
"Gotcha!" crowded Vesper.
He had shot down a black crow from the air. The
crow's dead body fell right in front of him.
Blood was pouring out of the bird. Vesper poked
the crow, which was looking quite prim. He
seized his camera from his backpack and took a
photo of the corpse. And though he was amazed
by the photo he had taken, corpses of crows
weren't a legendary finding on the internet.

Occhiolism

The full moon was shining brightly that night. As Roc lay down on her cobblestone bed, the memory of the splatters of blackness restarted the fight. It was a human who had shot down her soft friend. Despite the fact that she disliked the crow at first, Roc couldn't understand how someone could intentionally kill. The tales the clouds had told her were all true – sadly. As she looked blankly at the wall, an idea came to her mind. She had once met a witch in the forest who lived in a little cabin down the lake. Roc had no knowledge of the human world despite the stories of the clouds. It was rather a bothering struggle for her ignorance than a vengeful anger that made her get up in the dark to seek for that witch. She soonly arrived at the witch's territory, after she had flown over the bridge. She entered the rusty cabin without knocking. The witch was sleeping in her chair, snoring loudly. Roc gently touched the witch's arm, which made the witch jump awake under a second.

"How dare you enter my domain?" the witch exploded.

The witch was wearing a green dusty dress and a
tall hat. She had short blond hair which was flat.
She looked younger than a tree but older than a
ladybug.

"Well, a crow friend of mine was killed by a
human," said Roc softly.

The witch frowned and showed her impatience
by tapping her fingers on the table.

"And what do you want me to do about that?
Bring your crow back to life? Make that human
suffer?"

"I want to cure humans."

The witch bursted out in laughter. Roc gave the
witch a fierce look.

"You're serious? Well, take this then."

The witch gave Roc a necklace with a key on it.
The key was bent and looked useless.

"Only this key can end cycles, such as that of
human behavior. But never let it get into the
hands of a human!"

Even before Roc was given the chance to ask
any questions, the witch had kicked her out of
her house. Roc wasn't able to understand human
behavior, she knew her perspective was narrow.
The complexities of the world were still forgein
to her, and she knew how small she was
compared to all there was left to explore, yet the
key gave her hope that her perspective would

somehow widen soon, and make her life less a bore.

Sea

The second story Roc had been told was one about the sea. One day a human sailed the sea with a small boat. The human endured the high waves. The sea noticed the strength of the human and was amazed. For the human's strength, the sea gifted the human three treasures: a golden starfish, a four-leaf clover and a see-through trident made from a very rare material called plastic. However, humans used the gifts as weapons. He sold the golden starfish, which was brutally eaten by the new owner. The human threw the sea-through trident in the sky which then spiked a turtle, beginning the plastic pollution of the sea. Lastly, he kept the four-leaf clover, but instead of using it for anything good, he used it as a lucky charm during gamble games.

Fitzcarraldo

Vesper peered into the night sky and was blinded by the moonlight. He sneaked back inside his house after having been in the forest for the night. He was not satisfied with the photos he had taken. He slowly opened the front door, trying not to make any sound. In the dark, he carefully walked the stairs, yet someone was waiting for him at the top of the stairs. It was his father.

He grabbed Vesper by his arm and dragged him to his room. His father's grip was firm and painful. The yelling made Vesper feel rather shameful, making the scratches turn into bruises. And at last he was alone, the words had been harsh and damage had been done for which reason his eyes were rainy. His tears gradually moved through his eyes like an ocean of fire, until the fire burnt the eyes shut into a deep sleep. Inside the darkness of his eyelids colors appeared, dancing in one another. Spots of light turning like circles, gradually moving from one color to the other. A bright red color of warmth changed into a dancing bright fire that moved up and down like wings – like wings of fire. It was an image in his head of a girl with wings of fire, horns like spikes, teeth like needles and eyes like an ocean. Then Vesper opened his eyes. He had seen someone in the sky. He had seen a monster.

Sonder

The sun had risen. With the key around her neck, Roc flew as close to the human world as she dared. On her way, the clouds warned her about all the danger she could encounter. "They will slice you open." "They tell lies! They cannot be trusted!" "Death is the only thing you will encounter when you show yourself to them." At the edge of the forest, behind a bush, Roc secretly watched the humans passing by. She analyzed them. She saw a tall man wearing a fancy suit passing by. He had a grumpy look on his face. Roc thought about the man's life. He wasn't a happy man and tried to hide his feelings with anger and disgust. On a bench an old woman was sitting, reading a newspaper. Roc couldn't explain but the old woman looked like someone to trust. Roc hid her wings and approached the old woman.

"Hello?" Roc whispered.

The old woman turned around and cried out in fear. Within seconds the old lady had fled. Roc hid once again behind a small fence next to a building. She saw many different people walking by: a woman with her dog, two girls laughing with each other, a boy on a skateboard,

an old man coughing and two lovers. Every
passerby somehow made her realize how
complex humans actually were. All of them
lived unique, different lives, with friends, family,
ambitions, dreams, fears and worries all being
part of those lives. However, that realization
didn't comfort her. Humans were fragile, to cure
them a miracle had to occur.

Rubatosis

A monster lived in the forest. If he would succeed in taking a photo of it, he would get a lot of fame. His name would be worldwide known for the discoverer of the fire devil that lived in the forest. The image of the monster was constantly on his mind, too much on his mind, because then he hit a street light.

"Watch your step!" a man with a fancy suit scoffed.

"Kids these days are constantly on their phones," grumbled an old man, even though Vesper wasn't even on his phone.

Then an old lady bumped into Vesper.

"I'm sorry madam," Vesper said.

"There is a bloodthirsty monster with wings after me! Run!" the lady screamed.

She ran on. Vesper however went as fast as he could towards the monster, following the way the old lady came from. Yet, there was nothing. The monster had probably fled back into the forest. Vesper ran into the forest. His heartbeat rose fast. The excitement Vesper felt was lost in the sound of Vesper's heart racing. He noticed his own heartbeat. The rhythm gave Vesper an unsettling feeling. But as he was aware of his heartbeat, he was unable to take his mind off it. The gloomy lullaby of his heart couldn't be unheard. Vesper was still running through the forest, but instead of hearing the leaves rustling, Vesper heard his heart booming, "I'm here, I'm here, I'm here."

Ophia

There were many tales about the oldest well of the forest. The old well had long ago been built by the first human inhabitants and was given as a gift to the fairies and angels. Wells contained water, water cured life, and so wells gave life. The old well was what was going to bring the world a better future. Roc reached for her key and tried to speak to the holy well.

"Dear old well, this world seems broken at some times, but with this key the cycle of war will be forever broken. The cycle of pollution will finally end."

Roc leaned forward and took a look at the water at the bottom of the well. But just before she knew it. The key got snatched out of her hands. Roc turned around and saw a young boy – a human boy. And then he pushed her. Roc looked into the boy's eyes and into hers. His blue eyes were intense and his pupils were glittering. His eyes were unfamiliar, he was a stranger. His pupils were ones of a liar, but his iris was one of a trustworthy person. Eye to eye , she met the boy in just three seconds, making her feel vulnerable and confused. His stare with his watery eyes made Roc uncomfortable.

Nevertheless, she kept looking into those watery
eyes, until darkness separated them as Roc hit
the ocean bottom.

Nodus Tollens

"Click," peeped at the camera. There she lay in the deep dark well, a demon with wings of fire. Her looks were disturbingly uncanny, but her eyes were glinstering like those of a human. Vesper had made a photograph of the monster. He pictured the fame he would be getting. His mother with her green juwel proudly clapping at him as he's on stage, telling the story of how he encountered and overwhelmed the evil demon. Vesper stood with his head held high, with his camera in his right hand and a key in his left hand. He analyzed the key. It looked like a broken twig. He tried to get rid of the key, but it was stuck in the palm of his hand.
"What's happening?" he stuttered to himself. The key melted into his hand as if it became part of his hand. Vesper noticed how the sky color was changing from orange to blue to black in just a few seconds, and back again. The sun rose and went under in just a breath and brought a strong wind over the land. The sun rising and going down accelerated like it was a roller coaster. But then, it stopped and the sky ended in a dark purple color. The sun had gone down, as it appeared. The moon was firered and increased

in size until it exploded in a thousand shatters. The shatters were glasslike and poured down like snowflakes, however, the moment they touched the earth, ghostly hands emerged from the ground. Vesper agreed that his life didn't make any sense to him anymore, and not because of the fact that the moon had just exploded, but because the path he obligated himself to follow, the path that he thought was going to bring him pure happiness, had only brought him despair, as if he was in the wrong story – a story he didn't want to swallow.

Cold water

Cold water,
imprisoned the lava in ice blocks.
Cold water,
stronger than air, Roc was losing it from the
clocks.
Cold water,
froze a fairy, a bird, an angel into grief.
Cold water,
dimmed the wings of fire, made magic leave.
Bold slaughter,
the cycle of misdeeds ended.
Bold slaughter,
had lost the battle from cold water.

Lachesism

In town, Vesper was surrounded by chaos. The ghostly hands emerged from the earth and dragged people with them into the ground, into the earth's bottom. The world was consumed in darkness, trapped in the cimmerian shade of earth's clock, stuck in hour thirteen. Vesper felt the adrenaline rising in his body. He wanted to be struck by disaster, as if that was going to make him feel alive. He felt a strange desire to be dragged down into the ground, not because he wanted to die, but to experience something new that would bring him forward in life, to begin a new chapter. An emotion he had felt before, in the past he had dreamt of surviving a plane crash. Even though Vesper wanted to be engulfed in disaster, it was still an awful sight for Vesper to see the townsfolk getting dragged away by the enormously large ghost hands. Wearing her necklace with the green juwel, Vesper saw his fearful mother for her life. He ran in her direction and called out for his mother. Unfortunately, a ghost hand came before him and snatched Vesper's mother with it into the ground, leaving Vesper all alone. Disaster had struck him, but it was different than he had

imagined. He had lost his mother, and an
unearthly disaster had occurred. The flames
were higher than the eiffel tower and he wanted
to step right into the fire, yet he did not.

Nightmares come true

He just wanted fame, to be known and to be not useless.
She just wanted a better world, to change bad to good.
Fire and ice, so different but also so much alike.
His life was trash, he was realistic and chose for himself.
Her world was bad, she was an optimist with a hopeless quest.
She had a dream, he had a dream, but neither came true.
Only the nightmare was strong enough to set through.
Days passed in the lands of fear, she was still in cold water,
and he hid, all alone in the forest, a lonely deer.

Ambedo

Vesper sneaked to the well, trying to hide from the ghostly hands. He took a look inside to see if the devil with wings was still there. Yet, he couldn't see in the darkness and decided to climb down. It took longer than he thought to reach the bottom. He was shocked when he felt nothing else but cold water at the bottom, the devil was gone. He looked up and saw a white hand reaching for him. Vesper accepted the fact that the ghostly hand was taking him with it, but instead of taking him down into earth's bottom, the hand made from clouds took him up into the sky, all the way to the clouds. The fluffy clouds were extraordinary in the dark. The hand took him through the creamy clouds. It felt as if he was floating on a sea of pillows. He felt safe in the cloud. Ultimately, Vesper saw her. Standing on top of a cloud stood the monster. Yet Vesper didn't see a monster nor a devil this time, but an angel with wings of fire. He was lost in the details of the creature. She had no fangs, but beautiful cloudwhite teeth. Her horns were curled and cute. Her wings were literally on fire, giving a feeling of warmth like one you would get coming home from a long walk in the cold snow. The moment Vesper looked into her watery eyes, a tear streamed down her cheek and then the hand let go of him. Vesper fell down like an evening star, and in the end his world turned dim.

Air

Lastly, Roc had been told a story about air. It
was the last element humans had to betray.
Humans and air had never been good friends.
The tornados and humans had been at war for
centuries. So one day, a man went over to the
cabin of a witch. He bought a magic potion
which would poison the sky, pollute the sky, so
rainfall and wind would cease to exist, so the
humans could win the war from the tornados.
And before the clouds were able to stop the man,
the magic potion had already been released into
the air. Humans were taught ways of polluting
the air. But instead of weakening air, the potion
and pollution made the life in air mutate into
new aggressive forms. Thunderstorms, even
larger tornados and heavy rainfall were the
results. Thousands of men gathered to fight the
tornados, but none of them survived except for
the man who had released the potion in the air.
The tornados offered him eternal life if he ended
the war. And so he did. Peace between air and
humans was promised. Yet, as soon as the man's
eternal life began, a tornado swallowed him.
And for all eternity the man was trapped inside,
spinning around in the large aggressive tornado.

Humans had betrayed both earth and the sea, but air had backfired